Blood Atlas

Luke Morgan

BLOOD ATLAS

Blood Atlas

is published on 1 May 2025 by

ARLEN HOUSE
42 Grange Abbey Road
Baldoyle
Dublin
D13 A0F3
Ireland
Email: arlenhouse@gmail.com
www.arlenhouse.ie

ISBN 978–1–85132–334–0, paperback

International distribution
SYRACUSE UNIVERSITY PRESS
621 Skytop Road, Suite 110
Syracuse
New York
13244–5290
USA
Email: supress@syr.edu
www.syracuseuniversitypress.syr.edu

Typesetting by Arlen House

Contents

ACKNOWLEDGEMENTS

Acknowledgements are due to the editors of the following in which poems, some in earlier versions, first appeared: *Abridged, Bath Magg, The Cormorant, Crannóg, Cyphers, Fortnight, The Irish Times, Poetry Ireland Review, Magma, New England Review, New Hibernia Review, Orbis, Pirene's Fountain, Skylight 47, The Stony Thursday Book.*

To Geraldine Mills and Nithy Kasa, for their early encouragement and generous endorsements.

Special thanks to David Gardiner, Deirdre Curran, Jenn Pond, Robert Morgan, Jake Morgan, Maria Morgan, Martin O'Carroll, John Morgan, Eileen Humphreys, Niall Humphreys, Macartan Humphreys, David Curran, Ann Curran, Paul Curran, Molly Twomey, Aideen Henry, Lorna Shaughnessy, Rachel Coventry, Mary Madec, Connie Masterson, Emily Cullen, Annemarie Ní Churreáin, Victoria Kennefick, Aoife Lyall, Sarah Clancy, Jessica Traynor, Kurt Rosenberg, Zach Stevens, Hendrik Harms, Kirsty Gregory, Colin McNamara, Eamonn Wall, Jackie Roantree, Eddie Connolly, Ciara Wall, Noelle Lynskey, Seosamh Duffy, John W. Sexton, Megan Merchant, Cormac Culkeen, Mary Tighe, Brian Curran, Jim Curran.

I am sincerely grateful to the Arts Council/An Chomhairle Ealaíon for a bursary which enabled me to devote the required time and attention in creating *Blood Atlas*.

for my grandmothers

BLOOD ATLAS

One Day, Blood

One day, blood makes a start –
creates its own vessel, steps out from the sea
on a journey it takes towards a heart.

It crosses the borders it draws on a chart,
circles the globe carelessly.
One day, blood wakes with a start

to find it is doomed, and so learns the art
of setting down roots, community –
a new step it takes towards a heart.

Then, of course, things fall apart.
It takes to the boat to flee.
One day, blood makes a new start

in distant lands, hauls bricks from a cart,
puts up scaffolding, grows its family,
lamenting its exit from the heart.

But blood will return – it always outsmarts.
Blood hears itself echo, heeds its own plea;
for each day, blood must again start
this journey it takes towards a heart.

PART I

LONGITUDE

Long ago, navigators determined latitude by
designing tools to map their ships with stars.
But longitude without radars
was a mystery – if you travelled west quick
enough you could complete the trick
of keeping a sun unmoving in its sky.

Stars have always used us as their guide.
They move in one direction, we hurtle with force
in another, each vying to meet on a course
we only get half-right. Lovers cross
continents, unknowingly part of a coin toss
until by chance they collide

and light makes of itself more light.
I can somewhat trace where I am, I think,
with the latitude of lineage, paper and ink;
I got here by Margaret Coyle, my North
Star, and Margaret Keane, my South. What thwarts
me in uncharted night

is the route I've yet to fulfil –
should I row much faster, or stay calm
in answer to that confounding qualm
of keeping stars from disappearing
because here I am, fervently steering
to hold them up there burning still.

Blood Pressure

Like the Corrib, the Danube and the Seine,
ambitious ancestors are restless and loud.
When I tune my bloodshot ear
to its own throbbing histories
I hear castles, science, the pen.

My Ulster Keanes nearly had Dunluce
long before Queen Elizabeth turned
the rim of Rathlin Island vermillion
with scores of warring men.
In Birmingham, the Mitchells knew
better luck with a steel nib; they made
enough to put themselves in Chateau Impney.
There was James Prescott Joule then,
inventing new units of energy,
inscribing his name on the packaging
of every edible product. My grandmother
sold lace gloves to Grace Kelly, and when
it came to operating on her brain,
a fellow Keane wove with the scalpel.
Grandpa led a school in Monaghan.

Unless I move, I'll become a stagnant fen.
I feel their blood gather in me, vying to shape
the expanse beneath my writing hand –
a river that will not stop until
it proves the memory of itself right again.

Prayer to James Prescott Joule

Dear Joule, the last time we met
we were the same spark-spitting gene
inside a single body; we split
and became water, air, heat, water again,
until you struck life, underlined your name
on our shared blood atlas, your legacy
an Aldis lamp you carried beyond death
to await my distant reply.

Dear Joule, it falls therefore to you
to hear this prayer; grant me the energy
you proved cannot be extinguished –
only passed from one form to another –
to persist, to love again the vocation
I've given my name to, rediscover the clarity
which once changed the air around it
like a signal light in the fog.

Meeting with an Unknown Ancestor

Aunty, you will survive your famine –
how else could we be meeting now
among our doubts, blackened as potato shoots
under rain only the Irish sky
can sustain without revealing how.

I'm not here to regale you
with our leaving and returning tales –
of creaking mines in murky seas
or cousins who left us on the steps of
orphanages with no birth details.

I am here because you are the proof
I have endured all this before.
Witness my hunger, Aunty, tell me
its thrumming will not be my unravelling.
I need to hear you reassure

that it won't yet make an animal of me.
I haven't come to see how you get by –
how you chew bog oak until it turns
iron-bitter like blood from a blister –
I've come to be reminded why

we must inherit a bruise, keep it safe
without hiding it from the world,
become the kinds of custodians
a pain bigger than ourselves deserves
so we can pass it on one day, pearled,

into the skin of someone still nameless,
who has our nose, the rift
in our chin, our pockmarked tongue,
someone who, like us, won't be ready
to understand it is a gift.

You doubt that I am real, Aunty,
but know I hold your life inside my spine.
Our realm is in-between, like rain smoke.
I can prove you will survive your famine;
please teach me how to survive mine.

Gift

I am one sixty-fourth a man I've never met
who only has his dad to saddle with the blame;

who only has his dad to saddle with the blame
for passing on the traits he always feared he lacked;

for passing on the traits he always feared he lacked,
this man forgave his dad, and left him to his airs;

this man forgave his dad, and left him to his heirs –
an act of love for one he could not know of yet;

an act of love for one he could not know, and yet
his own father thought this boy would never grow;

his own father taught this boy who would not grow
to know the gift of blood and live in gentle debt;

to know the gift of blood and live in gentle debt,
I am one sixty-fourth a man I've never met.

Field Marshal Montgomery

I wish he wouldn't
but it's half-time, so
my grandfather rubs
dust off a ledger, traces
a handwritten lineage
to show me your name.

Commander of the *Desert Rats*
during the war, we blame
you for trying to crush the Rising
and cast you on the team
we long to crush today.
Driving to my mum's clan

I cross the invisible line
along County Monaghan
six times in ten minutes,
clench my teeth
at unfamiliar road signs
of a land once removed.

So, Montgomery, distant cousin
of mine, as the match is resumed
and we call for England's scalp,
you remain my inconvenient tie,
my grim claim-to-fame,
a surname from an old shelf

that reminds me how
my blood attacks itself.

St Patrick Issues Me a Warning

Stolen one day, forced from the home I'd made;
that's my beginning. Welsh, like your surname,
speaking now for Ireland, hoping that you at least
will stomach a warning.

We are tribal. People will claim their acre,
war around you. Long before land was green,
it teamed with blood – a colour which stays the same
despite where it bleeds from.

Don't forgive me – I also learned to rule
the soil no ancestor of mine worked in handfuls –
stood above the pagans below, invoked
new gods to defile them.

Here's our dormant fate – to give way to hate
you must believe the seed's not inside you,
waiting, silent, seething, growing when leaders
order "scorn your own neighbour".

Listen, poet – your grave plot's as green as mine is.
Snub my scripture – blood's neither mud nor water.
Own your shadow. Always remember you're
a traveller here too.

A Ditch in Hallow

Here lies – almost – the eternal resting place
of Tessie Mitchell, marked when she leapt clean
off her bike into shrubbery to escape
the ripping up of bullets from a Luftwaffe plane
on the road between Hallow and Sinton Green.

You struggle to replicate that thrill,
the nearness of not having a name.
Any lane can seem insignificant until
the pen, like a ditch, underlines it. The days still
ahead of you take their faltering aim.

MINE

My grandfather was only a boy
when he took to an Irish Sea
littered with mines from the war
to meet his grandfather,
Worcestershire's pride and joy.

This man had cut them off.
Marrying a catholic in those days
was laying a charge
made to sink a lineage. But
death had made the old man soft.

My grandfather could have refused.
Into that dimly-lit room
he walked, the ailing man
planted a kiss on his forehead.
And all was defused.

A View of Chateau Impney

I spy its coloured spires fleeting between trees,
turn off the motorway and ignore the *Private Property*
sign until some steel bollards halt my descent.
Now it is completely hidden, this house
of my great, great, great grandfather, leased
by the Salt King in the years before the war.

I've asked my grandad; the details are a haze.
With my dictaphone I watched him trying
to bring names and dates into focus, this grey-
haired man who I struggled to unblur.
The smell of his house was vaguely strange.
He obliged my questions with the polite air
he was known for on company boards – they
still had him answering calls in his 80s.
Once, I called by his double-gated
home, but he apologised down the phone,
said he had a memo to phrase.

The chateau is now a hotel, says Google,
closed down for renovations.
I sit in the forbidden carpark and ogle
its grand architecture through a screen,
imagine its carpets, shades of old world hue.
Another time, I lie, and turn out of the drive,
the manor not so much leaving my rear view
as having scarcely been there in the first place.

Congestion

At a hospital in Kathmandu
the patient shows his disability to me.
Attempting to thank him humbly,
I think of my grandmother in the days
she could only utter a single phrase
after her stroke. I'd stand, on cue,

embarrassed and waiting
as words got lost in her frontal lobe,
leaving us to sift and probe
what she was trying to say,
a stuttering panic in her way,
my patient grandfather translating.

Dad said she was once tall and grand,
a woman of quick wit; but at the table
I avoided eye contact, feared the unstable
twitch at the edge of her lipstick,
petrified that she would pick
a moment to suddenly demand

I look at her. The Nepali who
has lost the use of foot and hand
now struggles to understand
what I'm trying to say to him.
So, I repeat her phrase on a whim
and hope it will still ring true –

"It is lovely to see you.
It is lovely to see you."

A Brand-New Cap

My great, great uncle William would drown
trying to save it from the Boyne –
his brand-new cap, like the one upon the crown

of my head. On his way down
to Sunday Mass, neat as a sprung coin,
my great, great uncle William would drown

when other conniving boys in town
claimed they were just toying,
seized his brand-new cap crown

and threw it in the river. With a frown
he waded through that darkened void –
my great, great uncle William – to drown,

become an anecdote, a morbid noun
our family struggled to fit a boy in,
a gap which brand-new caps would crown.

But like a river of renown,
memory's a current we can join –
so that my great, great uncle William won't drown
I retrieve his cap, wear it like a crown.

GRANDPA'S VOICE

The snow falling in Knock, County Mayo tonight
is like the static behind my grandpa's voice
on the audio recordings he made in 1984
with his parents; the soft patter of their gossip
leaving no home in Clones untouched
until the whole of the Newtownbutler Road
is made new again in my mind;
once-familiar chimneys, shed doors
and branches sacred under a dusting
of memories not known until now.

I haven't heard his voice since a crowded room
in 2010 when somebody reckoned
it wouldn't be too painful to hear him sing.
After the whirr of the tape's rewind,
the silence we bowed our heads to
as his trembling, imperfect tenor
climbed the notes in *My Lagan Love*
was wider than any mass that day. A cry
from my granny broke, playback was snuffed
and I lost him for a second time.

Outside, each uttered flake
fades the night back to greyscale; the street
forgoes its car brands, telephone wires
and neon signs in pursuit of a timeless peace.
I close my eyes, remember him reading
notes of encouragement on those first poems
I'd attempted, shared with no one
except for him, his voice coming through
the phone receiver from a faraway hall
like gentle magic, like snow.

Ancestry.com Ghazal

I asked my granny to spit in a vial –
a hanging line as long as the Nile.

From Drogheda to County Monaghan –
she fit a lifetime inside of each mile.

The town whispers only spurred her on.
No one in Clones could match her style.

Her chin protruded whenever she'd chew,
whenever she'd cry, whenever she'd smile.

She left, of course, before it arrived:
a map now even more worth the while.

Though we found no secret, no lost memory –
her lineage grows, single file.

Her people and mine came from the soil
that fertilised this revitalising isle.

Nosebleeds

My granny has only so many nosebleeds left in her
we've started naming them
like Met Éireann name storms –

Ruth stays tame all weekend
but comes gushing when
the mink coat whispers in the wardrobe.

Martin can usually be expected
by afternoon, rages how
she's a case for more professional care.

John is countries away
at the back of her caruncles,
could turn up suddenly
in the middle of the night,
cause her to trip on the carpet.

Mary's efficient, leaves no trace,
arrives dry and barely visible
beneath the nostril rim.

Lee's forecast around the clock.
Dominick's blotchy but warm.
Claire shows the others up
by making tissues pirouette
in the loo basin
like ruby-quilted dancers –

it's a wonder the woman
isn't just skin and bone by now.
She keeps on leaking us from herself,
while around the house her crockery
trembles with the sign of first wind.

MUTINEERS

Peggy's a mutinous spirit.
She sought purpose as a locum
in nineteen-sixties Monaghan
while having seven children
whom she punished over a lifespan
for loving her. One was mum.
She'd never admit it,

but mum'd mutiny the phonebook
if she could. It's her blood
that made me work in the arts,
declare war on an ordinary life.
Like Magellan, I quashed upstarts
in my head who said I'd no good
chance, spurred on by the luck

of a granny who chanted my name
on the winds. We've all
reached success, a kind of Finisterre –
Peggy's was Gran Marnier in Toulouse,
Mum toppled a President's Chair.
But this same rebel gall
always finds a new captain to blame;

back from conquest, alone,
it goads me now with my own choice.
I hear them rising, these mobs of doubt,
accuse me of not being content.
Peggy's gone. Mum's got hers to figure out.
The only orderly voice
to drown them out's my own.

TRUE MERIDIAN

Like the convex longitude of Earth
destinies are never parallel.
My ancestors set out from random birth,
encircled oceans in a caravel
until their conquered worlds were neatly sundered.
Before I was a pupil in an eye,
I was both the Viking and the plundered,
exiled and returner, famine cry
and starved. In +1/-1 degrees
I seek my true meridian along
the passing lines of strangers, try to please
my host of gifted dead so I'll belong,
still yet to find that one defining *I*
we learn to measure all our journeys by.

Part II

A Brief History of Blood

This story begins with blood
or the running away from it;
chased by my brother's spit
over a floor strewn with clothes,
falling, face first, my nose
gushing thick maroon mud;

hearing mum's sullen warning
the winking razor in the bathroom
wouldn't hurt, and when the plume
opened in my small thumb,
realising, eerily numb,
she was right; the morning

I fainted during school,
knowing the only way to shed the shame
would be to move towns, blame
dad, who, when I banged my head
on a beam, distracted me from dread
while pressing tissues to hide the pool.

Years later, watching a drone
slice my fingers dazed,
pretending to be unphased
for my future wife
after I plucked it from the sky; my life
is defined, I've always known,

by the times I'm struck with force;
when I remember, in the shock
before it gathers, I am a lough,
a reservoir full to throbbing brim,
only ever a ripple or whim
from returning to my source.

PIMPLE

Back when you would quiver
just by talking to classmates,
it was a kind of superpower
being able to shoot blood
across a bathroom mirror

until in all the dabbing
you saw a recording dot
blinking clean and regenerating itself,
urging you towards the performance
of a special young man, grabbing

to become student president,
liked by both bully and teacher,
but whose pores would clog
to frantic white, take years
to squeeze and burst again.

BLOODLETTING

"I'm going to take some of your blood,"
the doctor says, as though I'm not
the artist people swore I'd be
long ago, but an organism
capable of endlessly
replenishing what it has lost.
The needle drains its flood;

I study a blemish on the wall
and remember my school trousers
with crusted stains on grey
after the first girl I properly loved
emptied me down an alleyway.
Where did that young Morgan go?
I heard someone recently recall

as though those other fluids –
sweat and tears – do not count
and we should only be defined
by what can be extracted from us.
I feel faint. Legs inclined,
the doctor puts me lying down
and, in the way of old druids,

lays a hand over my pulse
as all the time I feared
I'd wasted, the hope re-built
in the sole of my foot, the love
I was sure had been spilt
arrives tumbling back around
to meet me all at once.

Bad Blood

During the days we shared an artery,
we could be arguing in different parts of Galway
but still catch the rhythm of each other,
at intervals we remembered the cathedral
and the rush from a text that read
I think I might love you.

Since our rupture, the town's been stained so long
the copper dome looks blackened;
even the seagulls don't care anymore.
Still, I feel the negative space
left by an old pulse
every time we pass one another
on the Salmon Weir, or Prospect Hill;
startling you out of your headphones
with polite eye contact, then filtering you out
for a day, an hour, a minute.

If we were a pair of ICU beeps
we'd look like this:
one spike waving a crap *hello,*
the other mimicking a steeple,
piercing the sky until it has
no rain left to bleed.

Clot

I keep it under a cardigan sleeve,
this throb knot, purple roadblock,
humming through my boring excuse
when I'm asked about the family thing.

Older now than when my dad had me,
I shy from this sort of grown-up talk –
maintain a long distance, avoid loose
socks on a plane, secretly planning
my panic for when a close one conceives
to start the wind of my nine-month clock
out of their lives, a pitied recluse,
the uncle who only gets a ring
because he's alone on Christmas Eve.

I try not to think of the vein that's caught
in my elbow's shrinking noose,
desperate to reach a hand that inks
out names on a family tree.
This, it warns, is how to stop
a bloodline – not a botched cannula's abuse
or a compression sock's tight cling –
but stubbornly choosing to believe
staying still will unravel a clot.

Sonnet for a Deer Tick

for Jenn

I love you, darling tick, because you remind me of the trade
required to enjoy the land with just my skin, a truth
true since days of holy wells, where, to ask for aid,
you had to give something to the stone, a ribbon, proof
you knew the cost of healing. So, darling tick, to you I offer
the well behind the bone circle of my elbow;
drink, unravel my blood with a whisper, I prefer
this intimate toll to the shock of any short, sharp blow,
and though you caused a panic when I learned of your thirst,
I realise that without you, being with her is only heaven,
and what's the use of light when there's no shade first?
You are the reminder if we get lost in one field, or eleven,
we must return to the altars of our bodies, newly sure
in the search for you, we will gift touch, find our cure.

Leeches

They fall from the sky here, we're told,
climbing through trees to the leprosy hospital
where knobbled clay and painted blinds
spell the miles from Galway like heat from cold.
On our phones is a video by our cameraman, full
of giddy horror at a gentle leech he finds

near his heel. The picture wobbles as he tips
salt onto its back. A few moments of calm
where you wonder if the salt thing is just a myth
before blood blooms from its lips,
bursting slow like ink from a dam,
appalling all back home we share it with.

A doctor gives us the tour. Patients smile and *namaste,*
press fists together for the westerners,
not knowing why we're here, or caring;
it's lunch hour and they're getting on with their day,
demonstrating balled stumps when he refers
to them in English, numb to our staring.

We're here to make a film, raise vital funds.
Half of us try and blend in by ditching shoes
which is how we were found by our famous leech.
We'll gather our footage, swap our suns,
spread awareness of this place, choose
to believe all we regurgitate is speech.

PITCH FOR *THICKER THAN WATER*

I have this idea for a screenplay: one day, the UN severs
all familial ties on Earth, and people are free to choose
relatives. Our hero, estranged from his son, endeavours
to re-apply for the role of *dad*. But then, he hears news
that his son has already filed for a new dad – a teacher,
sports coach, a friend's dad – and this breaks his heart.
A plot twist occurs midway through our family feature
when he considers where his own father is; the old fart
is in a nursing home somewhere, staring at a dirty wall.
So, our protagonist enrols as a janitor at this facility –
a montage shows him cleaning shit along a narrow hall
until he starts to steal moments of confused tranquillity
in the old man's room, joining him to study a wall stain
shaped like Dún Laoghaire's pier, where, one morning,
the old man forced a 99 on them to numb a silent pain.
The film ends as the son from the start, without warning,
turns up with ice cream ... but real life isn't that breezy,
I know. I just like that this dumb little script could allow
three troubled men to admit they could have gone easy
on each other, without knowing when, or knowing how.

Blood Brothers

for Seosamh

Do you remember, Seosamh, bursting
a blood vessel in your left eye
while we were still at school?
You showed me under blinking streets
the dawn our absent dads met
for the first and only time,
and as they laughed in the rumble
and sway of the old Volkswagen,
you explained how you'd thrown up
and all the heaving popped something,
soundlessly spreading deep dark red
over the white of your sclera.
You walked the halls, a scarred marvel,
so at ease with all who stared.

When you came to convince me
to go up on the stage with you
at the talent show that year
and perform an excerpt from
Blood Brothers – the scene where they
cut open their hands to shake
on it – I made an excuse,
knowing you'd upstage me.

Later, your dad's funeral.
We got a flight to Newcastle,
sang some songs and stood shoulder-
width over a hole in the ground.
You hadn't really known the man
but still braved the church spotlight
to read a poem for the scant crowd
and I watched you, fighting back
tears thicker than any blood.

PILLAR
for Nithy

not the Aenid
spoken start to finish
in the ballroom of the Listowel Arms,
the air so thick
we could move it;

not the ice cream at dinner
while you shared your troubles,
stirring as though
it was your responsibility
to keep things from melting;

not the plucked cello
as we sat up there by the jacks,
our clandestine giggles given power
by the highbrow verse
we were late for;

but the pillar in the corner
you laid your back against,
your hand on the carpet next to mine;
the one doing nothing
except holding the entire ceiling up.

A Vision as Atlas

Mornings like this – coffee in bed, dappled light
through the elm, a good book, schedule loose –
are heaviest. You pick a fight with Zeus
and he curses you with holding up all this
love. Sudden visions of those you'll miss –
your brother, immobile, that terrifying sight –
you, the grim sentry at your mother's bed
awaiting some inevitable news –
what you'd say if the quartz-like fuse
faded from your lover's eyes
for you to suddenly realise
all the times you never said
how grateful you are she's in the frame.
Oh, I beg you, titan, first cousin of mine,
turn me to mountains so I can become the spine
of the world. These heavens are bright and weighted
with all that has passed and is fated
and someone, somewhere, is calling my name.

Hypochondria

There is a surgery I visit
every time I imagine losing you.
"The chill is at your back again, is it?"
the consultant sighs, scratching a new

notepad because the others are all full.
I prove to her the sleep I've lost, the rims
of my eyes where blood turns purple,
ask how I'm supposed to keep my limbs

from feeling out in the dark of a room
to confirm you're still there, constantly,
and in the reaching, forget themselves, consumed
by what they'd do in tragedy.

"Don't you think this is a question for
a therapist?" she asks, unqualified
to explain where the mind goes. "I'm a doctor,"
then reminds me I've survived

these thoughts before. But this, I stress, is an illness,
a virus whispering through my veins,
weeping from me as sweat, witness
the velvet dread that loving sustains.

"Take one a day," she'll then intone,
handing me a blank script, her case unfought.
I'll leave to fill its white alone,
write about you standing there, then not.

The Last Bathtubs

They're getting rid of bathtubs, mum,
which means every day, I'm further from the door
upstairs in our home in Sruthán an Chláir
and truly knowing who you were
on the other side of steam I was sure
would emanate ad infinitum.

No more can I see the water you were in,
left until morning in case the suck
and gargle would wake us up.
I try and take each chance I get
to immerse in scalding tubs, let
your blood rise to the surface of my skin,

but renovations drill on and I keep losing you,
mum; how you blink your tears away,
or laugh when plans can go astray.
I'm losing Epsom salts, candlelight,
the nub around your nails you bite,
like suds dissolving from my view.

They're getting rid of bathtubs, mum –
your thumbs are puckered and creased.
Mine are heading that way too.

Distributary

In this estate, the truth flows close to ground
like blood under an ankle's subtle knoll.
If someone wanted to get right around
the source of you, you'd take them on a stroll
up past a creek and through the open slit
of Duplex window, where you sit and read
your Mum and Dad's old letters on their split.
As both pens underline, and nick, and bleed,
your veins expand. They're no longer your own;
they look like his but coloured by her blue.
Listen. Outside, water meets a stone.
A river also trembles inside you.
You let it separate to live, bereft;
one half goes right, the other half goes left.

Circulation

The world has turned so cold these days
that we must fight to hold on to our toes –
frostbitten mountaineers, absorbing ice
up through our heels to keep it from our hearts.
I mute a close friend's argument of how
in any conflict we must pick our side;
remembering my parents – two people
I wished would stay in love, for I loved both
and both loved me, a circular conundrum
like a colour wheel, where orange can
not border blue, despite how well they pair.
I curse this love, but it's the reason why
I haven't yet gone numb, succumb to feel
this complicated earth beneath my feet.

A Poem is an Open Wound

A poem is an open wound –
weeping in silence, hidden in sight,
proof of a life that has moved.

Red, if we hadn't already assumed;
blue until it comes to the light –
poem, you are an open wound,

violently useless, lovingly doomed,
you protest with all of your might
how pain takes a lifetime to prove.

Your sound is a scream, fine-tuned,
you haven't run dry, but you might.
A poem is an open wound.

Those who can't hear you are bruised
and toil all alone in the fight –
some pain takes a lifetime to move.

Until such a time let's conclude
that surely as day follows night
a poem is an open wound,
proof that a life can be moved.

A Graveyard in Luxembourg

Before the screening I'm whispered in by mausoleums
supervising the street near the Ciné Utopia.
Most are old, their names foreign – Schmitz,
Mersch, Becleese-Beck, Roth, Fritz –
some are not – by the marble angel, I see a Mc.
Carthy from 1988. Today, I've heard French
and German, sure, but learned of Luxembourgish;
soon, in the theatre, I'll hear Gaeilge, its guttural flow
like dew rolling down a leaf. Our gravestones, though,
lack the confidence of these – each a hench
temple, more tall than wide, built for proud folk
of a tiny country who brought dialect up
from a bygone century, replicating the flight path
of a dandelion which, in the absence of wind, asks
a mouth to help it survive. All is smoke.
There's been no wind for quite some time.
I wonder if anyone will attend our miniscule
film, imagine Galway dialogue landing
on empty seats, bolster myself, understanding
we may have already passed our prime.
I lift my hat, bid these quiet plots a *slán*,
return to the rosy loneliness of travel.
Beyond the wall, weeds reach up from a ditch.
I hear the sound of an ancient language
try outlive the stone it's carved on.

Beloved Artery

Beloved Artery,
if I ran out of words
what would become of me?
Like migratory birds,

if I ran out of words
I'd scatter into air,
like migratory birds.
Would anybody care?

I'll scatter into air
with my anxiety.
Will anybody care?
Recurring mystery.

With my anxiety
I can be clearly heard;
recurring mystery
when I run out of words.

I have now clearly heard
what would become of me
if I ran out of words,
beloved Artery

The Day the Sea Froze

The day the sea froze
I was on the prom
feeling faint from a blood test.
I didn't believe the tide was slowing
until a child nearby pointed,
yelled, "look!"
I moved to the next bench
to check it from another angle.
The spindrift winked at me
like glass in my grandfather's cabinet.
A dog bounded out
to catch a crab
hanging from the crystalised froth
and, one by one,
we all took our first careful steps.
I knew it wouldn't break –
safe and cold as a tomb underfoot,
more stone than any Burren.
There we were: colour-coated dots
sliding across a great slate mirror.
When at last I looked back
the shore had grown darker.
I watched headlights flow down hills
and replenish themselves
like this heaving breath of water
I thought would never stop.

Part III

The Lesser-Known Senses

1

Proprioception

(n.): the sense of detecting where your body parts are without having to look for them

It seems like any normal town – grass spine
along the bohareens, rope knot thudding
off a cattle gate, rain gushing
out from a gutter spout – but you notice
a house that wasn't there before; a path
blurry with the signs of subtle growth.
All you wanted when you walked these lanes
was to have written books, yet here
you are again, checking these roads are still
how you imagine them, feeling the knee
jerk from a faded traffic sign, seeking
reassurance from the shedding trees
that you still are who you think you are.

2

Nociception

(n.): the sense of detecting pain

On a day you bonded over cobwebs
your dad explained how we have more than five
senses. Proprioception: even if
you were blind, deaf and dumb, you would still know
how to find your toes. You listened, then
excluded him over the next few years
from birthdays, graduation meals, events
where he was nowhere to be seen or heard.
But like a twang on silken thread, you knew
his loneliness across each continent,
pictured him in rooms pricking himself
on photographs which showed you, growing.
You long to go back, tug the direct line
between you two, show it hurt you too.

3

THERMOCEPTION
(n.): the sense of detecting changes in temperature

You're cleaning cobwebs up and down the wall
when you discover tiny metal hooks
from that December you sought to enthral
her with a Christmas from the storybooks –
you hung a string of lights around the room,
conducting her amazement into heat
which kept away the brunt of winter's gloom.
Today, the warmth between you is discreet.
You work together to repel a flu
with rubber gloves, while your apartment wheezes,
two cups of steaming lemon sigh at you,
the conversation tapers off and freezes.
These hooks are rusting, but you leave them in –
removing them would grant the cold its win.

4

Cardioreception
(n.): the sense of detecting the activity of the heart

She leaves, and electricity cuts out.
You grab a torch and follow every vein
until you find the fuse box. Nursing doubt,
you reassure yourself it's just the same
as years ago, when you would push the trip
valve up through clenching teeth to simply spark
the building into life again. This blip
you might not fix – Massachusetts' dark
and lonely lawns begin to weigh on you.
Is there a future you can see with me?
You hear her voice, though she is out of view.
The work before you get down on one knee
is bringing back the lights of No. 1,
like windows that once caught all of the sun.

5

MAGNETORECEPTION

(n.): the sense of detecting Earth's magnetic field

But then another woman's message thread
flows against you, with you, to you, through you –
this latest somebody with eyes as wide
as amber doubloons. You've been here before.
This time, you try and push away from them,
appearing only motionless, stuck
in cowardice, despite the major fight
of magnets begging you to turn around.
Deep down, you know that quick and easy *snap*
will not attract the prize resistance brings
and so, against the poles of your nature,
you pull towards a less convenient
version of yourself, a stiffened eel,
a blackened tongue defying every current.

6

HYGRORECEPTION

(n.): the sense of detecting moisture in the environment

Yet one wet day you almost fuck it up.
You start by taking couple photos down,
removing fingerprints before a crime.
A rain-wobbled reflection keeps you guess-
ing what you will and will not do. They're here.
Your face is melting. Whisper the right things,
get what you think you want. You stop their hand
to keep a line uncrossed. It all ends there
but in your underwear a moisture swells –
this grim insistence of anatomy
to weep an animal from high ideals.
Your kitchen sweats with thick and humid shame.
You see them out and open every pane
but condensation on the wall won't dry.

7

EQUILIBRIOCEPTION

(n.): the sense of detecting balance and acceleration

October. Orange light and static rain.
You're stuck in traffic, held between Nepal
and Worcester; two eventful, high-octane
adventures stimulating your morale.
Last week you almost drowned in quicksand; next
you'll win a glass award and make a speech.
You check your phone again in case a text
comes through to bring excitement back in reach.
The branches of Woodquay provoke the shore,
you wonder if you're even moving. The GP
checkup's looming; that fear-inducing chore.
On the echocardiogram you'll see
the line that you must learn to daily stride –
between each jagged low, each jagged high.

8

Electroreception

(n.): the sense of detecting electricity in the environment

The hues that resurrect the sky from night
are not St Elmo's fire, but a span
of pylons, lightning-struck and out-of-sight
from where you're watching in a campervan –
her jiffy pop, familiar and adored,
a promise of the gossip to be spun,
some scrabble pieces strewn across a board
from games well-fought and others soon well-won
– these pleasures will be yours, but they can wait,
for here in Gort the puddles glow despite
the rain you hide from yet appreciate
as each new fork and epileptic strike,
like a camera flash, delivers thrill
and keeps you grounded there, together still.

9

CHRONOCEPTION

(n.): the sense of detecting the passing of time

The tannoy from the airport tombolo
signals evening. You're on Inis Mór,
sequestering the time so tomorrow's
like Ros a' Mhíl on Conamara's shore –
within reach but far enough away.
Your heart was broken first time you were here,
but eight years on, it's all worked out ok,
a to-and-fro just like a tide that's near
and throbbing loud is suddenly not there.
Where did it all go? You're to blame –
so distracted you are not aware
of how the fading light transforms the plane.
Your work's not done. Could motivation sour?
You blink again – the clock loses an hour.

10

INTEROCEPTION

(n.): the sense of detecting the internal state of the body

In the days after the endoscopy
you drive inside the small hours to reach
a place explored in childhood. All is still.
You stop your car and step into a night
unencumbered by a prying streetlight.
You know this place just like a diagram –
the spleen-shaped lake, the crooked hawthorn tree
distorted by the winds, a traffic cone
from when the council foolishly believed
they could tame these rural marshy hills –
but now you cannot see a single thing
and though you hear the beat of your own breath,
it returns to you from a vast terrain
which you both know and, suddenly, do not.

About the Author

Luke Morgan was born in 1994 and currently lives in Galway. Arlen House published his debut poetry collection, *Honest Walls*, in 2016, followed by *Beast* in 2022, which the *Irish Times* acclaimed as showing "a real ambition ... with striking, energetic imagination." *Blood Atlas* is his third collection.

In 2025 he is the recipient of the Lawrence O'Shaughnessy Award from the University of St Thomas.

Luke is also part of an award-winning Irish filmmaking duo, Morgan Brothers, with his brother, the composer Jake Morgan.

www.ingramcontent.com/pod-product-compliance
Lightning Source LLC
Chambersburg PA
CBHW021237310126
38773CB00005B/24
* 9 7 8 1 8 5 1 3 2 3 3 4 0 *